Towards

BY E. A. MARKHAM

Poetry

HUMAN RITES   1984
LAMBCHOPS IN PAPUA NEW GUINEA   1985
LIVING IN DISGUISE   1986

Stories

SOMETHING UNUSUAL   1986

Editor

HINTERLAND   1989

E. A. MARKHAM

Towards the End of a Century

ANVIL PRESS POETRY

Published in 1989
by Anvil Press Poetry Ltd
69 King George Street London SE10 8PX

Copyright © E. A. Markham 1989

This book is published
with financial assistance from
The Arts Council of Great Britain

Designed and composed by Anvil
Photoset in Baskerville by Wordstream
Printed and bound in England
by Morganprint Blackheath Ltd

British Library Cataloguing in Publication Data

Markham, E. A. (Edward Archibald), *1939*–
    Towards the end of a century.
    1. Poetry in English. Montserratian writers, 1945–
    Texts
    I. Title
    811

    ISBN 0 85646 223 3

For my grandmother 'Miss Dovie', 1867–1953,
my mother and my sister, Julie Hill

ACKNOWLEDGEMENTS

Some of these poems have previously appeared in *Ambit, Artrage, The Caribbean Writer, Cross Fire, Delta, The Literary Review, Numbers, Poetry Durham, Poetry Review, Prospice, Race Today, Samphire, Stand, Verse* and the anthologies *Hinterland, The New British Poetry* (Paladin), *The Penguin Book of Caribbean Verse, Tibisiri* (Dangaroo Press), and the Harrogate International festival brochure, 1988.

CONTENTS

PART ONE: *Towards the End of a Century*

Towards the End of a Century / 11
New People for Old / 21
A Challenge / 22
The New Season / 23
Rendezvous / 26
Spare Part / 27
Epitaph: A Match / 28
Pause in the Game / 29
Next / 31
Coming Out, Older / 32
Part of the Landscape / 35

PART TWO: *Family*

Mother & Son / 39
Another Son / 40
Grandmotherpoem / 42
A Family Gift / 44
Herstory / 48
The Grieving / 50

PART THREE: *Poems for the Occasion*

The Broadway Thirteen / 55
Olympic Winner, 1988 / 56
A Poem for Peace / 57
A Sentence to Write / 60
Land Behind the Mountains / 62
From the Building Site with Love / 63
This England? / 66
Another Footnote, The Same Text / 67
Familiar Man / 69
A Marker for a Poem on This Subject / 70

Self-Portraits / 71
Long Lines from the Island / 76

PART FOUR: *(Counting the Letters of) Love*

Love Song / 81
Letter to a Lover, To Be Treated with Suspicion / 83
Leaf / 87
Rewrite / 88
Nibble, Nibble / 89
Beast on Holiday / 90
The Father's Story / 92
Love in the Hospital / 93
The Mother's Tale / 94
Looking Back, Ah, Looking Back / 96
'Little Fellow' / 97
Covering Up / 98
A Poem of Experience / 101
The Thing Not Said / 102

NOTES / 105

1 Towards the End of a Century

Haiku: 'Les Chênes du Vilaron'

After the concrete
a partner returns to paint
olives on the wall.

Towards the End of a Century

i

My hand is steady:
This, my friends, is no mannerism
From an adopted land. A mother's mother
Instructed us: *Do not grow old*
In a place unkind to you. This brought
Me back. The hand
Is no reek of manliness,
More the hint of some little way to go
Before words serve their sentence
To a final full-stop. Look, madam; look, sir:
Bless all who are gathered together in this
Non-holy place. My hand is steady.

Some who are confused
shift and turn away thinking this trick unworthy
of folk who declined a life abroad:
a hand not for shaking, free of gifts, unmagical.
A trick, like the boxer early in the century, taut,
plucking a fly out of air.
But not this, not here. You turn away,
right, perhaps, to be insulted. Some buy time
(for the hand is steady) till it be urgent.
Who will tell us when it is urgent?

ii *a*

She wants to know his colour
the blind one, black or white:
what is he wearing today?

And we say to her:
think of things nearer your age,
think of not seeing as your blessing.

She has outlived, out-thought us,
she will not play:
priest's coat or surgeon's:
what is the butcher's colour today?

Because she is blind,
because she's now the daughter
of her daughter, punishing, punished

we listen. Through her
they have deprived us of sanity,
they have aborted our line

of argument. And we, near death
are patient, huddled
with those who wear our blood,

white coats
black coats:
how can we embrace them like family?
How can we make them clean?

ii *b*

Here is another part of the wood.
On a morning before we were born,
or later in the day, the year,
the thing we strive to recall
broke the tranquillity of this place.
None can remember when it ceased
being sacred. Some still worship here:
the barber cutting hair, the dentist
pulling teeth; others in from the sun.
(The musician and the dancer try to remind us
of what is lost – but they are outside.)
The travelling merchant gains audience
of sorts. Some sit, a few kneel. And over there
bodies are being bared as if for healing.

And in he strides without guns or bombs,
without words that hurt, that kill:
how is it done? He's ridiculous –
a blind man approaching sex with a stranger,
alert both to charity and to ridicule:
he is not ridiculous.

The musician and the dancer enter
to restore with memory time before pain.
We do not know how to dance to this music.

If we fail some will come
and hold a conference here
next year, each year
for years.

iii

We bring you news, of course,
From a far country. Bearers of gossip,
We have been moved on because
This late in the century, all
Have heard it. Safety in numbers, we come
With no more hope than a messenger bringing bad news
To Cleopatra. Some who have perished
Have been unlucky in their audience.

I bring you news
Not from obscure military men who force you
To mispronounce their names;
Not of mountains of skulls stored
By the last government, displayed by this one, used
To confirm theories, to discredit us all.
I bring no more news of slow, painful death
Of a people ... we have had this
And have not used the knowledge.
So I bring you something manageable: this
From a far country not at war. Yes,
Fires have been lit in the house of your family.
Bullets in the backs of childen have stimulated
Debate. For us, at the end of a century,
Who wish to influence debate, the price is high.
Let us sing.

iv: **A Protest**

Even though it is this year, this century
and more of us are barren
and some who murder walk the streets
and are happy:
and friends grow shifty and turn away
from children (who have so long, so little
time to live):
and each of us can match a bad experience
told over dinner:
and glasses, dentures and other aids
now live with us:

Some resist,
like a casualty of this group
draining away poison piped into the head,
or get through the day without ache;
some who might preach a sermon from this text
and think better of it.

v: **On Another Field, An Ally: A West Indian Batsman Talks us Towards the Century**

for Malcolm Marshall and Michael Holding, resting ...

Into the nineties, into the nineties
Ten to go, ten runs, don't panic ...
Think Bradman ... never got out when into the nineties

Nerves of steel, drive them through legs
Beginning to buckle *think* the three W's *think* Clive Lloyd
Think Richards and all those ruling heads

On the coin of cricket. And relax. Now where am I?
Lost in the arms of voluptuous Anna. *Fin
de siècle*, recalling the days of immortal Kanhai

Hooking to the boundary from a prone position.
Cravats & decadence. Good ball. *Christ!*
Man in white coat weighing the decision

To point the finger, legalized gun
With power to run the 'Man of the Match'
Out of town. Not guilty. Not guilty, my old son

If I say it myself. A lapse
In concentration quickly repaired by nailing
The Will against any further collapse

This side of the century. Here behind the barricades
Stretching from 'Clifton' and Gordon 'Le Corbusier'
    Greenidge
Through 'homelier' architects of our days

Of glory – the team's Frank Lloyd Wrights –
Up against pollution, thinning ozone, treeless forests
In the tropics etc., each run lifts you to the heights

Of vertigo. And for you down there, Miss X, Mrs Patel
At the corner-shop, this wicket guarantees
Orgasms, guarantees that this last exile suits you well.

And damn it, I'm out. *Out?* There's no morality to this game.
Protesting genocide and burying your head
In sweet Anna's thighs, it's all the same.

The butcher of dreams, man in white coat
Offers no reprieve, his butchershop in Hounslow in need
Of more meat. Yet again I've missed the boat

Of the century. Breach in the wall.
Bowled through the gate. Marooned from the grand
Ocean liners: SS Sobers & Headley; not by formidable
    Wes Hall

Line of destroyers; no *chinaman* or finger-lickin' spin
To obscurity – just a *gift* with your name on it
Lacking spite, Physics or Philosophy, innocuous as sin.

Like I say, there's no morality in this game.
Protesting genocide or burying your head
In sweet Anna's thighs, it's all the same.

vi: **Face to Face**

1

my house shifts
like the loose tooth
of an ailing
monster.
I extract it
and we trespass
among the clouds
in unpolluted seas
through a road-map
of foreign languages.
Occasionally I return
to the monster
who greets me
with a sharp grin,
its rows of houses hurting
like new teeth.
What does it say
after years of learning
to speak?
'I am not yours,'
a grin? a grimace?
'I am not yours.'

2

he pauses to think
of his name carved
in a foreign wood.
It recurs this time
with a sigh on stern
lips of a too-late
wife. The after-dinner
joke under Provençal
olive spills wine

in its memory. And now
in the country of his birth,
the accusing, exhausted soil
the accusing, self-ripened tree
confront each other.
Branches wilt
as they must. Friends
help opponents to cut
them away and disagree
about what will grow.

3

the man peered at me across
his life and apologized
in a voice I have sometimes used
in private. 'Man, you leave it late . . .
to come back. The place gone down now.
Used to work your people's land
in the old days.' The disappearing patch
of garden, the orphaned fruit-
trees, the 'ruin' from a past
decade tugged my memory back
to childhood – so many buying the lottery
of escape. Here, what was shelved
gathered more than dust; the memory
put in deep-freeze on our exit, melted:
the power-cut a controlled accident.
Now the body of your time lies
ill-preserved, unaesthetic. Recognition rinsed
my mind and his face
like spray from a hose: he stood guilty,
the bright lad in the class giving
the wrong answer, prickling us with hope
and unease. Now his face, furrowed
unlike the land, is an error no one
meant. I owe him tribute, like the land.
I bring him comfort in my news.

'I have been reading the endings of novels.
I have celebrated with strangers
"Solidarity" in their struggle.
I have been consoled by friends
In their paid-for homes,
And have observed the final shape
Of their families: I am whittled
By their need. These are the old films.
You have seen it all, they say;
How it works, what to avoid: you
Are the envy of us all starting out behind.'

And I vow to do things differently,
To start afresh, to deny the weight
Of my experience. Of our experience.

New People for Old

Here the sweeper, there the pick
in the hands of a prisoner
removes evidence, stain from the pavement
of those who lost this game before you.

Elsewhere nature covers with snow,
with ice what no Court of Law will see.
You come struggling past guards unable
to call your bluff of youth:

the defence learnt by heart – responsibility
for children, parents, *self*
is not needed. So you put down a marker, markers;
settle in the house of murder

and decline to change the name of the street.
Those beaten, raped, robbed here
will be vindicated by your life. Normalcy,
not return to innocence is the aim.

And it works, draining the threat from old dreams.
Till they come again, figures
from a time long buried. They have come
like an illness we can't treat

striking the least protected as always,
matching blood with that long washed from pavement,
buried under snow. And blood proves
thin as water, as the monuments will show.

A Challenge

(Who said it must end here?)
The hymn fades out: they look up
from their knees at her,
loose-flowing, a tightness
of flesh or tension, mocking . . .

Dead lips can't speak her intention.
Embalm. Put him on ice. Anything
till we work it out –
the match of Will and Chance, body on body,
two colours in one lifetime.

She comes in as to announce
the war has ended, supplies are through:
there is Logic in the world.
She is lived-in (O God) naked
under her clothes, unconsumed.

The old, repenting, are ready
for ceremonies that flatter them (how luck
still seems like virtue!). With rings
on young fingers, back stern as a rebuff,
she must renew her challenge with better arguments.

The New Season

i

Now is the time – after the riots, after wars
of which you might be part –
to pause at the side of the road clear of rubble.
You have helped her across: the child
reaching for your hand has grown a claw –
a joke to let you know
that time has passed, is passing through your lives.
Tortured by natural cause
she is too frail to spurn a hand
that might be friendly. In what is left there of mind
your threat has passed.
You stand at the side of the road fearing
that something which has many names is lost;
that talks round Peace Tables;
terrorists – some with prop of ballots – who mangle sleep
mean less now in daylight
than tribal skill to cross a road
without help of the hand you might not like.

And you cross trailing something,
not like the shopping, more like children
from an outing, weary and ragged, halting the traffic:
you drag this autumn branch of resolution
bit by bit shedding last season's certainty.
Bells, telephones, screams break the lights
reminding you of more than the street.

ii

Amnesia, like a bloody history, forces this season
to relive its past. So my trip is willed.
Back sometimes to a house of youth to view
replacements – slow-moving, defective and accurate.
Why is this necessary? My *fact*
can be denied, a casualty of memory
like the trick of editing out a nation's butchery.
This attempt to make me try harder must fail:
the upstart comes confident with our energy.

In another house without threat I breathe relief
without relief: how good, how good.
Books pile up, shelves outgrow the sons
of friends; outgrow fertile daughters adding
to a stranger's tree, branch by branch . . .

When, I ask myself, did they cut you down?

iii

A popular game in the right season:
the grass is green, is green . . .
Bouncing the ball, something unphysical
makes you falter.

In the park you missed the ball.
New blotches on the skin are mouthed
with a mission. Accept it:
in earlier versions you are dead.

iv

Innocent of how things work, she looks
this way and thinks: the chair has wheels.

And thinks: when the children moved house
the old fart couldn't get up the steps.

And thinks: I like this game.

v

A new partner is promise of a warm climate
where joints unlock by slow-moving magic:
there among fruit and vines, fingers
restored by earth, by sap
attempt to relive their past. Indoors
a letter, much forwarded, brings news
of the world (remember that pleasant couple
who visited?) It says here – is it possible? – he hits her.

*

We are here.
We are under blue sky
enjoying the new season. The cloud
of pollution which must fall somewhere
falls somewhere.

Rendezvous

And she must dress carefully, dress well
For this encounter with a stranger; the children
Will be fed, put to bed: someone will read them stories.
At home they say she has a lover.
She goes past shrines where the faithful stand
And wait – for a Mandela, for news of a family,
In respect for those freakishly dead –
In spite of the logic of men in uniform.
She goes past them, keeps going, refusing to think
How few things can be accomplished in one life
As lived by her; composing
In her mind letters to some who must doubt
Her love. And, beyond that, more . . .
Is this where it happens? She is not unnerved by her
    affliction.
Today, she is *taken* with her consent.
Back home, there is no complaint. The children
Are fed, she is put, gratefully, to bed.
How clever of others to live her life, take the stress?
. . . And now again we see her dressing carefully,
Dressing well for a rendezvous.

Spare Part

... Unlike the 'boy' in Trinidad who built his own 'plane ...
like a fellow-spirit in another century
wheel in hand, tiny spring on table, staring
at the clock put back together
mocking the pedantry of its first maker;
or like something nearer home, the TV comic
who conjures *table* from a packet with instructions
and stands, left-over wood in hand
(and a partner glowing with condescension) – like this,
but with no sense of discovery
that things without their parts work well enough
(or who would be standing, walking, *loving*
who had borne the skill of surgeons?) Like all of these,
like none of these, like something yet to be discovered ...
O, paint me a song, sing me to distraction
show me that springthing in life that doesn't work.

The jokes still puzzle, no escape
from routine amusenent of a family
who won't indulge inventors at the breakfast-table.
Till he calls their bluff
and empties a room of what was never treasure.
This too-sudden act of dispossession awakens
the house at night with cries, with noises new to him:
margins have been eliminated at our peril ...
That things were never what they seemed
even when they seemed so, was a point he might have made
more gently. But a partner, for years, had heard
the cries, the pleas of house
for its lost bits and pieces and had not gone mad,
had not moved out not woken not murdered him –
this brave or stupid woman,
this part of the house that works, works.

Epitaph: A Match

Tennis: it is summer
In England. We know names of players
Enough to have a preference

Deeper than the favourites.
Though we are unlikely to dwell on upsets
At Wimbledon. The good times

Outrank this. Something blinks,
Blinks out of control
Till we get it back to where we are.

Tennis stars, old pros
Defending turf, are a quarter-century
Younger than they were.

Exchange of gifts convinces us
The good times are over. They come
Wrapped in tissue to bolster

Marriage, children, years not matched.
Summer in England still. We replay
Points throughout the night

Self-conscious as body language
Served as jokes – too tired now
To recall the score.

A Pause in the Game

... And so to clear my head
I wander off, from time to time
letting recognition of the familiar
bring me back to consciousness:
in this corner of the universe
things are clean and orderly, people
more beautiful than I remember them.
Here's a little party caressing
books not stemmed glasses
which the scene recalls. I know this
to be a place of gentle torture
where the well-favoured come
with lips and teeth clenched
to suffer the English language.
In time, they go away, unmutilated,
new capitalists of the Word. Why
are they still so beautiful?
My greying, yes, I've thought of that.
And yet, though sweetened by youth,
some of these come rank
with what we have purged from ourselves,
with what their parents took to war. How do we
know them? The end of learning here,
as elsewhere, is perfection of disguise,
not change of mind. Surely,
some wandering moralist with a knife
must mark a face, carve on it a sign
which spells contagion. In defiance, face
after face turns towards me taunting
its immunity. Till I see her.
Yes, I'm awake, I see her. Brazen with scars.
With this unexpected honesty I fear
a stage-manager, a thug in control
of the street bored with matching violence
to money. The victim holds my gaze
a second longer than her colleagues:

what is her parents' curse, so rash
to appear? I conjure conventional
cruelties, the stuff of headlines, visions
Macbeth-like on the heath, of a line,
flawed, down the ages, to warn
that evil wears its own face; our age,
though cynical, is not unmoral. And I pass on
hearing the beautiful people giggle
at my innocence. Out of sight, I accept
as criminal father the motorcar partying
towards the crash; or an old cooker
flaring like an angry dialect you least expect.
By the time I get to street-prowling-
moralist-with-knife, I begin to lose
the faces, in random rooftops, in branches
of a tree. They are far behind now,
slow-crunching those tell-tale
words we pass around, like eating
an apple in company, wholesome if not quite fun.
Silly to make of this little scene –
removed from the game in question – so much,
with others elsewhere monitoring my return
to clear-headedness. I can see them
pacing with impatience. I can see them
dozing with relief.

Next

i

in the queue

from one day to another
from the public servant
the oiled tongue of the confessor
the soldier at war
from she who rapes easily

from another false start in bed
an uninvited birthday
a parasite in your mirror

from a convinced majority
a judge in drag
a political fire going out

from the 'not prejudiced really' surrounded
by those 'quite like us really'
from survivors predicting doom
from the uninitiated among conmen
from one failure to another ...

ii

next
in the queue with
a five-year plan
or a free election ...

Coming Out, Older

i

Like my friend from the village who wished
to write a sermon, I vowed
to live to *twenty*, despite premonition,
and thrilled to the challenge of the next five years.

They passed soon enough in an acne
of exams and girls
showing favour to others: now we are facing
the opposite direction looking back
at what might have been missed.
Who doesn't read in the eyes of a stranger
recurring statements
that hint at a bargain you failed to keep?

Some land on their feet, friends settling
for more than seemed possible –
second families thriving in the sun
(reading Krishnamurti, sharing privileges . . .
and this towards the end of a century indifferent
to succession). The issue today:
how to express love to a son too heavy to be carried,
too big for the breast?

Ah, but there are the rest of us; a colleague
investing in blackness
waves success like a policeman armed
with an in-joke.
I do not resent this, we validate each another.

Women, still more promise than threat
have sent one (or two) of their number
to allay fears, to arrest me with kindness
– a prudent thing to do kindness

– now it's your turn kindness
– we're not getting any younger kindness
even – I can't live without you kindness ...

ii

The world is full of sermons,
of men whose mothers never sang to them when it mattered,
whose daughters punish them with guilt.

Here is a look-alike
finding *root* in Public Transport:
his railway-ethic prevents the world falling into confusion
(Paris is the place that smells of cigarettes.
Far-off Toronto reeks of innocence.
The National Museum of Art in Lagos is marked on
    the map ...)
How they get on, other people, with neglected parts
of my life: next-door's blackman
and his milkman find accommodation;
one sees a fascist who wishes to poison milk,
his restraint a tactic
soon to be acknowledged by the Queen.
The milk-drinker is a snob who takes whip to the enemy,
kissing the fingers of his concert-pianist under the
    bedclothes,
teasing the mouth into intimate things, words other than
    English.

Between *fifteen* and *twenty* (this is an old, old voice)
you collapse a decade dutifully
by thought, maybe by its opposites. Now you study
how to stretch *forty* to the full limit of *fifty*
without recurrence of amnesia, without the aid of surgeons.
You ponder the energy of a Macbeth choosing to go forward
    making waves ...

I number among my clones a Philosopher of Accident.
At *sixteen*, young and in possession of a car
he managed not to kill his colleagues.
Later, in methodical London, a stranger returned
the compliment. Then as a student
attending the factory where workers knew their lessons,
he offered his hand to a machine which ate fingers
(with discrimination, it declined – two cheers for
     prejudice).
Now he counts them all intact, adds here
or subtracts there a phrase or two from his Philosophy.

Too late, I think, to hide behind him, behind them.

Without sermon, without Philosophy, I look on
as the blackman next door and his fascist laugh
at the joke which they conspire to share
with me; a chance to come out
and surprise us all.
A chance to come out, older.

Part of the Landscape

The old English patrial would call it
a blot on the autumn of this isle:

thickening trunk built to thrive in another
climate; they were the makeshift

hedge; they were strays who paused
late at night while strangers in passing

cars assumed them to be local:
by morning, all would see better.

Maureen is known as the Lady M
living above her station; Philpot

fearing the decades making him androgynous
like Judge, like Politician, matches her

with elevated thoughts as a form of defiance,
his early vow to prevent that ugly

roll of fat sitting on the back of his neck
converting him to religion of faith

in Self, stretches his mind miles
round retirement: suppose, suppose

his situation were different, could he cope
with it? Would he blow it all by, well,

forgetting his Swiss Bank Account No.
and be ruined? Or would he write it down

and fall below Maureen's level once again?
This sudden chill of autumn with leaves

getting restless made them fear
nakedness under the tailored lives

of a woman with a cordless telephone
(taking her jury service seriously) and a man

planning anew to defeat cancer and the heart
attack, as he had done younger enemies. And

nature re-enacts the dream, past and present,
of things in the street, ripped off your back.

2   Family

Haiku: Things My Grandmother Never Said

ON LIFE

Don't join the circus:
all you have to protect you
is a safety-net.

ON TEETH

How to say Xian?
Your dentist never thought of
travel to China.

Mother & Son

She destroys him,
destroys him, the smile of his failure
softening her lips: not a surprise,
then, at this accident
on the way to other high-flyers
in the family. The pioneers, drugged
by altitude, so bad at knowing how
to land: they made for enemies'
safety-nets, got lost in the tangle
of arms and legs out of the straw, like the straw
but of surprising, lasting strength.
When the threshing stops the bed is made.
Some remain manacled, white collars
round the neck. She fears for this son;
lines on his face, a trick of movement
so like the first flyer, lost
in action, the ghost prowling far from home
fêted, they say, like a man.
She shifts the smile two decades towards
the edge of disapproval –
you can't reward failure of an exam.
Ambition grounded: what will come of it?
He must learn to go carefully, pick
his way past frowns, past obstacles
on the road. He must
walk through barriers that don't kill others.

Another Son

They have been led by attacks
in the area to expect ...

and now it's come: the brick,
a neighbourhood Art primed to splinter

midnight. Now all is quiet. No paraffin. No fire.
The *front line* starts at the brain's

sixth sense; so someone here, not dressed
must stumble from sleep, ill-armed

to defend what none has grasped.
And there it is – something familiar

of another universe long gone from this house. He stands
key in hand, unbelieving: he will not

come in from the dark. The family,
after this escape, re-forms, calls him

the familiar name. He has been abroad (he sees
them sliding down bannisters), he has not

kept track of what lives here. The key
to the door threatens to fit

a shared experience. He does not know
or will not say what country

he's been held in, how long before the trek
back; but can weigh brick, like this

against key, as in a foreign market
or a hostile neighbour. The mother looks

past his eyes and refuses to confirm
madness. She has been wrong before

with the family. For when he throws
his key, something must be done.

Grandmotherpoem

for grandmother Margaret, 'Miss Dovie', 1867–1953)

thinking many things, grandmother
I can't trap the memory, itself like a kite
to blanket us without coarsening our pact:
it is not cold climate, not famine relief that triggers this
    need.
Though more than the annual hat of fashion must clothe us
    in words.
So I put it off, more and more play the errant;
with dissecting verbs occupy this or that high table where
    the world lies bloated.

You must be asking when this apprenticeship will end?
Running & jumping, ball-games, preaching and Latin were
    early fantasies.
Now, wandering in a garden far from us, I step
on the wrong end of a rake
and crack my skull: the yellow scream of grandmother burns
    the head.
Surprise, a hint of things malordained, skids me past *us*
till embarrassment makes it safe: this is an accident.
A third time I step on the rake: *this is god!* 'Boy, wha
    happenin?'
I am at risk in the world. This is no accident.
Something leaking through my head has value.
It wines, it lusts, it fills empties fills my space.
Its logic meanders like a stone too heavy for the stream.
It heaves sense against sense cascading down the boneface
while the wet of mothermother drips into thimble: my
    bucket, my ocean.
And the kite is a cloud of badness dribbling, drizzling a
    parable.
From somewhere maleness spits defiance to hold soft matter
    in its rock of stubbornness

from the wreck, debris of grandmotherpoem
and a thing not recognized as fear of rakes.

Bits of me, long abandoned, floating past
jostle one another like strangers on a march.
The voice which breaks from its full set of teeth
comes like a uniform, polished: we are at risk.
Grandmother, grandmother, her bath over, smelling of
    bay rum & bible
knows how bad habits, like long years abroad, and the
    profession of maleness,
lead to ugly bumps on the head. So men must cover theirs.
In my hat, in a foreign garden, when the leaf is about to
    fall from its tree,
grandmother appears to speak to me:

A Family Gift

i

It must carry no hint of wreath.
The desire that it should be memorable
like that first grown-up party
or going to see the *Lear* formidable
not in ranting on the heath

but in mining tunnels beneath the text's
patriarchy, quelling debate
of mad and sane kings, good and bad daughters
is a rash displaying your own state
of disorder: she's not vexed

by these questions. We agree
something special is in order
for mother's last social outing
like one of us clearing a hurdle, a granddaughter
finally, of exams, breaking free

of a chain of whispers. Now we can display
our private Olympic team of sprinting,
leaping intellect in a Chinese
restaurant – all grandmother's scrimping
and saving rewarded in a way

less mysterious than prayer.
Sorry: let's call truce to these fights.
She will be our visiting dignitary doing
the rounds. Show her the sights,
and promise another tour next year.

ii

She is dressed in black
Smelling of camphor;
Not taking any chances
That she will come back:
So I make a joke about camphor.

Where to go? Art Gallery,
Restaurant or film? Thanks,
You give with one hand
In tradition of the family
And attack with the other: no thanks.

Church is out. Let's not get heavy.
How about a trip south
To an autumn landscape pruned
Of lizards, frogs – *gift-ready*;
And to bring water to your mouth

To bring back the pride of youth
Every kind of grafted mango,
Pear and sugar-apple:
But mother, to tell the truth,
You don't *have* to go.

She never learnt to fly,
Can't put herself through it
Without a cousin, long dead,
Who knew how things worked in the sky
Since no child of hers could do it.

For food and water take
Medicine, matching means to ends;
And secure safe passage from the war,
And good village people to bake
And cook and clean – like old friends.

This is what she asks of children,
And they talk and talk:
She waits growing into dress and camphor,
Thinks: maybe they're not her children,
The way they talk and talk.

iii

Too old to start a life, to learn a new address.
Brought here a prisoner or a bride
To this place old and immodest as a man
Gone soft in the head: why do they humiliate me?
Even pages in the Bible look different in this light.
Won't mention it, though; don't want a fight.

The old life is a dream of accident
To family, fire in the street; strangers next door.
This banishment is protection from having again
To witness putting a child's child in the ground
(She traps, spills a memory from the family's old animal
    pound).
The dog that keeps her company wants to marry; oddly.

So true. And for all his simple tricks
What use is Oskar? He doesn't type or iron or cook.
She laughs at that: why so easy to please?
I revive cancelled outings, *innerthings* over years
Of fastidiousness. Somewhere on the floor
Of my mind, a case not used on recent trips

Holds knick-knacks – a rug from Mexico, jade
From China – possibly for a mother. Awkward, though
Like announcing: today a man first put his foot
On the moon. She's never heard of that, she'd have me know
As if to make the world new again.
And was he family, this Armstrong, was he blessed

By the Reverends Wesley and De Lawrence? Tell me more.
In America a young Irish President – *heard it*
Heard it . . . and two of your sons, Walter and Michael,
Fell off the moon. But uncle Nasser got to Egypt
Not liking conditions on that other canal
In Panama. His house stands empty on our land

Along with others. Bills for repairs will ruin us.
And so they send the boy – always a boy –
From Corinth, from Legba, from Montgomery, Alabama:
   today,
They will abolish slavery, free the family
To conquer Poland and Russia; to parley
With the Pope – himself related to grandfather.

Though false prophets come with the true
Even here to *Dragon's Teeth*. And now they know
Which Africa is in crisis. Your cousin not long ago
Brought news that Talks somewhere broke down; the
   humans
Were at fault: abandoned at the Conference, trees
And animals in protest, vowed never to talk again.

And today we are in black, dressed. Our politics
Will not let us admit what this means.
Undelivered gifts will complicate our dreams.
Still, we are conspicuous in the landscape – not as tall
As green above the ground or dead under it.
But clinging to the surface. *Amen.* And aware of it.

Herstory

My name is easy to pronounce, isn't it?
– reward for being young and gliding
towards the heart of the world. History
of a family helped us to travel with travelling
as an option. Though we hoped, by luck,
to arrive somewhere. And after these thirty years'
sojourn, no one will say if this has happened.

Sons seemed designed to ease the travel:
we were young, could produce our own army,
could translate dreams into marks in the dust (a flight
of fancy which warmed some who shuddered in the ship,
    panicked in aircraft).
They say it would take time: we were prepared
better than ancestors. I forget
if they were right. Now, children have grey hairs
and rest between journeys.

And here I am, half by choice, visited
by family. I am at home, they say: others
with difficult names manage exile. My speech
is recognizable; grown men with casualness
of boys call me mother. They do it
eating grapes at my table; without comment working out
riddles at the foot of the bed.

And from time to time something stirs
in them, like the days before they were here
when we trickled in from the edge,
from the foot of a body whose face
was still in the clouds, with words primed to conquer
territory hard as this . . .
Now they come to avenge violence
done to a stranger – that far woman
separated from family; this man – this TV face –

exiled in his own country, hospitalized,
yet young enough to be photographed, for love
to have the old meanings ...
Their freedom is what these children
half-strive for. They are skilled in grand
impossible names, not like mine.
Too late for me to dissent. But children
have children: there's comfort in that.

The Grieving

FANTASY ON THE DEATH OF A FATHER

And they came; they had to come again;
they came by plane, by sea, on foot, summoned
to the house of anger and grieving ...
Last time was less fun than the time before with no one
    dressed
to preen. Outside, yard people with gifts and memories of
    service
interrupt their plan to augment lives and homes with this
    death –
with drawing-room chairs and a dining-room table,
with pots & pans to this or that stranger, the heavy
cassava-plate to a near neighbour (but the mortar without
    its pestle
and the ghosts of rotting timber would remain within the
    family).
So why did they come, children, grandchildren, cousins
their foreign accents and city-tempers out of place;
why did they come to this site long blessed
with grieving, pretending it would change their lives?

And they know why. For one or two
it was like playing truant from school, knowing
the summons would come. Easy to invent what was missed.
Some had ridden luck – that childhood donkey still
    disdained –
and hated others left behind with pride. The family
    carpenter,
a Very Reverend now, long absent from this pilgrimage
still stole the show. Hard on others: a son with glasses
    sprouting
from his face these thirty years, who had not gone blind
and was still allowed to read what no one valued.
He was nephew to the uncle who had shared his name with
    others
and had loved them; he was brother to the sister who had
    become Queen

of country and of herself. All had been misled
and had been brought here to repent
before others who had changed their lives.

So it was different now from other times of grieving
when a mother's mother still alive accepted
that these non-dead from food and other poisonings
were tribute to her yard and kitchens and to her magic
    years;
and those outside talked of yard-things lost to family
of something blended with mortar and pestle
that had kept the house intact, the spirits happy, forces
more terrible than enemy tanks and pillage off the lawns.
Outside the hymn is a chant of names of things forgotten,
unhurried, like something distant, as from the hills: the
    names
of rivers of the world half-learnt at school: would an absent
    Reverend
in the absence of the Queen of ceremonies punish the
    congregation
for this lay knowledge? For they have come to bury one
    whose *obeah*
is too strong for death, hoping it would change their lives.

3   Poems for the Occasion

Haiku: Violence on the Tube

Hand on my thigh. Strong
for a girl. Trains make her shy-
ness so hard to bear.

The Broadway Thirteen

In the library they stick up the score
    BIRMINGHAM 6   GUILDFORD 4

In this room the temperature's high, buzz
Like flies round summer goodies. Self-interest
Draws some BIG GUNS to the Party . . .
Like others, I thrust forward pretending to hang back.
On display are members of the famous BROADWAY 9, 10 . . .
    THIRTEEN!
So young; all woman (and a token man). I'll show them
Where I stand. I'm here with you. I'm UP FRONT. Look!
Can't catch her eye, though, any TWENTY-SIX of them.
Must risk another PASSWORD to connect with GRACE
& JULIE under pressure. A crude man mumbles something
    TART
And is immediately offered a Victoria under wrapping.
To join the game I juggle coins and keys and lob a RING
Deep into COURT THIRTEEN and hear her call DOUGHNUT
In my favour. All around me mothers & young sympathizers
Collect their STONEGROUND, WHOLEMEAL, LARGE BLOOMER &
DANISH placards from full-time activists: their exploits
Too good to be true, less like icing on the cake
Than the thing itself: MARZIPAN BOX and ALMOND RINDS,
CHOC FLAKES, fresh rolls and sandwiches –
In this High Street-politics gone beyond leaflets.
Bolder now, I order a French stick not seedy,
In plain wrapper – and she knows I am a *camarade*, reaches
Under the counter for what goes with this danger.
She is careful not to crack glass with the heavy OATH
You share, for under it are RUM TRUFFLES and one
    GOSSAMER
WEDDING CAKE draped in innocence. She welcomes
    contribution
To the Fund, but says the chocolate bullets are extra.

Outside, a new recruit. I tell her the score.
    BIRMINGHAM   GUILDFORD 4

Olympic Winner, 1988

Scorning delights of
Emperors Domitian &
Elagabalus,

Eton Latinists
& Lord Byron, swimmer – not
to mention spoilsports

from Webb (cross-Channel)
to *Great Trek* Botha – enter
Nielsen, Surinam.

A Poem for Peace

for Kevin and Margaret Magarey and family;
and to other poets reading poems for Peace

i

We are unready, we have not earned
the right to speak on our behalf;
but with luck have grown promiscuous with the time,
for it is safe now, always, to talk of Peace.
Forgive me, then, the unanswered letter,
failure to acknowledge some other debt
to a stranger whose face is lost.
But people, some known to me, are dying
and I must take time off to think of Peace.

ii

Forgive me, forgive us (turning
from the spill of drugs in a favourite city,
from those hospitals for the sane)
claiming to represent some who can't be here –
a trick of arrogance, the posture of fools.
Behind our fog you see him 'body broken,
mind looted: you see her whose injuries
are worse.' They will not be untortured
by our Peace. And so, a little naked
we run for cover nearer home:

> *A house like yours, unready*
> *for large decisions . . .*
> *A girl in nightdress has just learnt*
> *to tie her shoes. Like this. Like this.*
> *Soon, she will forget the hamster buried*
> *in the garden, and give up urging*
> *the new pet to speak. She will find*
> *some game less childlike than her mother*

who still must pause, taunting, weighing
this hand and that
to determine Right and Left.
You have vowed to teach her the difference
through the years – sweet years – of games and tussles
without end. And she, your slow, slow learner
must requite you (another late developer)
with old, with new confusing signals
from which you might claim to know the truth.

But we must pause here, and think of Peace.

iii

Stubbornly, some who survive coups, famine
– refugees abroad and at home – hope
(though by now they must know better) next year
there will be food. That makes it pass,
the mood that war, BIG WAR, will level all our fortunes,
will make life just. Others,
who may not be named, keep busy
dissolving barriers between what is mine and what is mine,
embracing life
burying their dead –
at night, some see stars still
not weapons.
They know of us
smile at us
feed us;
scrape the earth to an early tune
accepting its age, its danger:
they validate us.

Forgive me, feeling a little foolish
(avoiding the city's veins, those hospitals for the sane)
trying to give tongue
to a harvest not poisoned
to rains that do not kill,

to someone, yes, who has learnt to lace her shoes
and demands a larger world to live in.
For all, and from this fog of words,
I call for Peace.

Adelaide
chez Magarey, 8.4.85

A Sentence to Write

Outside his office they lost the war.
Inside his cell he met the wounded.

Assault on the bad habits of prisoners
left them with reduced rations, home-made sex

till the ringleader lost his right hand.
Elsewhere the writer's typewriter typed
something of this. Like a criminal

he fantasized about visitors, *didn't he?*
Sensory privation though new to him
was not, alas, new to him. He could

stretch out each whim for a day or a week while his eyes
held open: his sentence, present; continuous.
A friendly torturer recognizes

his status of voyeur, brings paper.
The paper is the colour of his cell
large as the light

Now he must write (what
did you do
in the peace

of the bad
old times?)

He must fill
paper

on pain
of

D
e
a

t
h
.

.

.

Land Behind the Mountains

VISIT TO ALBANIA, 1980

Bunkers and spring onions
Gang of 2½ million
Smallboned, shortassed (well-bred
Skinheads in army uniform)
Pickaxe & rifle

Heavy-bottomed Albania:
The hand of a child
Directed by committee
Scarring mountains in graffiti.
Bouquet in hand, Comrade Enver Hoxha

Beams down on all, kisses
Old women, fingers the young
On film. POPULI PARTI ENVER!
In Albtown's carless 'Lowry'
Squares, women in bright colours

(Home-made textiles) weave
Grey lines of men into tapestry:
A new design. Evening people at leisure
Without prop of book, newspaper,
Pets, tell Chinese jokes.

Shaded-in shop-windows hint
At mystery. Raw-faced flats
With TV curlers too shy
For postcards, brood
Behind curtains, unlit.

We are curious. Our guide
Has an explanation.
What do the people think?
Our guide tells us. Why are there
So many heroes? He tells us.

From the Building-Site with Love

i: **New Site, Spéracèdes, France, 1972**

a glance

the second glance is deliberate:
an approving nod

All this behind my voice
is beautiful

Words fit awkwardly into mouths . . .
. . . are cut away, trimmed;
they fall among the trees: bricks
on the site

Workmen bring bits of other houses

It begins to take shape,
the shape bothers us.
It's ceasing to be *this* house.

A foreign accent rattles
the window.
The world adjusts.

ii: **On the Redistribution of Wealth, Part VIII**

*On Having Had Objects Stolen from the Building-Site
of a House in Montauroux, France, 1988*

They were kind to us, they took
The cement-mixer, water-heater, working-boots, nails
And other odds and ends to do with sites;
They were like old tutors pricking our confidence:
They left my channels open to you, they missed
The music of the forest, which is here; the song of the
    river
Which is to come. I am elsewhere in a locked house not
    seeing;
The television is a trick of smoking villages.
A blink after genocide, someone well-groomed predicts
    the weather
(Yes, we are building a house; it matters if it rains
    tomorrow).
And then the whiff returns of you at home too intimate
For paper: there will be space for such luggage in our house
– Renovated, not new – to prevent it burning for the News.
That is too smug for what is meant –
Days when we spoke of the house not yet built,
Not like these others trapping lives too soon in brick,
Walls strong around silence, around sobbing,
Cracks that reveal what could not be told without *nakedness*;
A fortress, leaving you in possession of its keys –
. . . The rascal in the night restores something of our house.

Today, the 'find' in our *rustique* wall is not gold
But an *ugly* you would like. *Ugly* is older than house, than
    ruin,
Than anything resembling you and me: a stunted
Mutant, lizard, house-slave, lizard, dog-lizard – fish-eyed
Marker that something forgot, reminding me that this house
    can never be made new.
We didn't cut down the forest for it. The logged pine

Draws no more than a frown on the face of sanity. Oak,
    untouched,
Brings beauty back to your face. The saw is not bloody;
Burning leaves do not give off the stink of skin. And the
    oliviers
Trimmed, promising to bloom like second marriages,
Will outlive our unasked questions:
Are the good times over? Are we young or old?
And again I sit in a house not our house, keys to hand.
A Minister – of, is it Justice? – miniatured in the corner
Pronounces *crisis*, mouthing a cancer, a failure of the heart
At this or that stage of a house gone wrong;
And I am angry that something not labelled fear and
    hunger
Finds conversion in our house; angry
That these keys lock up what makes it like other houses;
    angry
At the theft of cement-mixer, water-heater, working boots,
    nails . . .

iii: **End-of-Job: n.d.**

from the road, a house
'nestling' as they say

among olives – yet casting
a shadow. A familiar sign:

solid, immovable phalanx mocking
your doubt. Another 'fact'

to overwhelm you? No,
do not accept it. The house

is new (we put it there). Approach
it with expectation

before it settles.

This England?

... guests at midnight
                    stopping
outside the house. The one
without the gun demands

her name and (through
an interpreter) tells Mammie

she's got nothing to fear
if she's legal.

Another Footnote, The Same Text

i

Corrupted, in harmony with the time
where journeys end before you plan them
and what is bad might yet be worse
for danger comes singly in a city
not being bombed, ravaged;
and crises far-off or hidden leave us space
to convict ourselves of generosity
to those gratifyingly in need –
we rehearse the calmer virtues, we perfect
introductions when we meet.
Here, a man not young approaches
danger – a girl on the underground,
not quite a child: is this why screams
prickle, sting commuters into battle?
Swords slide out of umbrellas, guns
from handbags and other makeshift tools
plunge this railway station into farce.
This is no Ealing comedy, but replay
of ancient war (the Emperor's men, the Pope's
mercenaries, thugs attached to every *-ism*
and to none descend on target). Here (nearly here)
rumour marked a *wantok*. Briefcases come down
like bricks, kicks convince the alien
to stay down. 'I loved her' was a feeble
thing to say.

ii

He dares not help. He looks
past the girl separated from a brother
whose hieroglyphs on moving glass
none could read from the platform.
Now, she faces the wrong way, shunning strangers.
The man, as if clutching a lifeline, jumps
his own train and hides in a book.
Lines begin to clear. Words make sense.
There are safety nets, three or four ways
to land without injured pride or limb;
to drain from the unexpected this vomit of fear.
By now, on a station left behind, someone
less vulnerable or more brave has risked
the obvious, solved a problem. These old wars
are not won with experience. These memories,
like necessary partners, will not desert us.

Familiar Man

You fake the necessary sense of humour.
They make you live up to it, family,
with sly references to feet and clay:
a joke as wife and daughter

press advantage at the dinner-table,
dream alternatives behind your back. You aim
of course to protect them from wits who,
unlike yourself, cap sad endings

with applause. You've become familiar,
a known thing, a fact about our time –
like a plastic bottle outliving us all:
where's the humour, then?

Today a daughter of eleven suffers exposure
by a man (they won't tell you yet
till something worse threatens). Teacher
and mother comfort her and reflect

that daddy, too, is like a man.
You sense at dinner a prickling in the neck.
Chill from the shoes spreads upwards
softening clay. The women you protect

will tease you, naturally, for it –
like a daughter's early drawings with
'The Lady Who Visited' in your place.
So, now then, did you hear the one about ... ?

A Marker for a Poem on This Subject

Lawgivers sniff at
the scent of voters
cross-legged and provocative.
The hanging Judge sits
in his juice determined
to bear the itch, the itch . . .
Bring in a man of meat for inspection:
he did in the park violate her . . .
With starter's pistol
he will run will run run
round the scented racetrack
for crowds to bay at. Legs unfreeze
and spread. The track bloodies
without complaint. Judge
begins to feel easy in his clothes,
in his seat. Human rights
have been restored. The raped
one stays raped.

Self-Portraits

i

His features
were not chiselled
cleanly. The rôle of hero

had to be postponed
till ageing
conferred the dignity

stray parent-bodies botched.
He cursed his blundering
casual gods

as if it mattered.
He survived to pretend
that it mattered.

ii: **Survivor?**

An internal complaint he couldn't
pronounce: he began to look

after his appearance, to polish
his shoes. He could have died

in a random private war to sighs
of what-might-have-been; or done the thing

more publicly in a group protesting
the cause, burnt out in a flash

of exposure and heroism: thirty years
later, his name on a monument.

Instead, he lives on as somebody's
uncle, known at this address, disguised.

iii

Challenging his destiny the bachelor uncle
Claimed anyone would serve him

For wife. That's why he deferred
To her – so young and forgetful and mean:

He was not liberated. Over the years he won
The encounter with a *Latin* disease translating him

Into English. He had hoped to reach the summit –
Anything from conquering Persia

With Xenophon
To becoming his mother's mother.

No point now in regretting sons and daughters
Who failed to absolve him from the status

Of *migrant.* And if paying the mortgage
In this land growing young and forgetful and mean

Got in the way of the plan,
His message to you, distant Queen –

Of Tehran of Moresby of Dar and the Caribs –
Is, that paying the mortgage with one of another clan

Is a good way, too, of fulfilling the plan.

iv: **Old Fantasies**

Meeting in the street she says: Excuse me
Aren't you the piano-tuner who can see?

Suddenly, my ears are sharp, my eyes bright:
I have gained the necessary inches in height.

Quick. Place her at the water-queue, racked by thirst
After your mains pipe has suddenly burst.

In another country I dial the wrong number: she answers
In spite of the world's Mothers & Sisters, she answers.

At the end of which life has of course changed,
A new mortgage on the world has been arranged.

Not that it was easy: *you are a difficult word to say.*
Then you can be my perfect lisp any day

Was the joke we pretended to find unfunny:
Sour-milk to the disadvantaged, while we served ourselves
   honey.

Yet, she was olive in the holiday-garden in Vence.
She was my favourite village in Provence.

Life of such sweet Chekhov, slow-reading Proust,
A post-vegetarian chicken coming home to roost.

Enough: we all know – like great Empires of the past,
These things are destined not to last.

Now the ear is far from C sharp, eyes not bright,
And I've lost again those inches in height.

v: **A Life in Prose: I Don't Know Where This Road Leads**

On the island someone, children, mark the tarmac: I
DON'T KNOW WHERE ... and after a gap of months or
years decide they don't know where ... THIS ROAD
LEADS. The diction, the writing seem suspect for children,
though I had not thought about it. Not till last night when I
found myself beyond this point on the road.
    ... Where vehicles change species. A car skidding uphill
passes through another, earlier specimen with clearance not
enough to make this possible. Though it is all right in the
end – till the next challenge rears. I am half-way up the road
on foot, road cut into a mountain, climbing. On the right is
mountain, on the left, precipice. And the road begins to
crumble, to slip from mountain into precipice, to narrow, to
disappear.
    Mountaineering, I climb to safety, to peeling mountain,
break my fall – from right to left – against sudden rock
thrown up, volcanic, from what was valley, saving me from
precipice, till I fall into another life.
    And there she is in a makeshift building on the ground,
like a nurse's home in some emergency hospital. She is in
bed, dressed, still in my life. Or she is packing to travel. I
reach for blankets of apology – my life's intentions, no solace
to the poor and wounded ... She knows the time she has
been celibate. There is a person elsewhere who treasures
her: what unselfrespecting madness makes her practise this
long abuse? She has been assisting nuns tending the
tortured from this or that régime. This is what happens with
a life on hold: you can fill it ... fill it with worthiness.
    And here, on the island, beyond where THIS ROAD
LEADS, I cling to what she is fighting, I offer myself.

*

So today I admit to a fear of heights
And decide to walk round mountains of my ambition
Till the gap between what is and what might be
Needs no bridge. Someone must pay for this, surely.
To stop me looking down the ravines of old dreams
Glass, thick as coke bottles, protects my eyes.
The world is cloud, I step forward, arms outstretched.
I go forth without fear, one of the plains people:
Bless you my children, bless you.
Something erupts.

Long Lines from the Island

He was of a certain age, the dad, convicted with due
cause to his room.
(Unlike an animal tied somewhere and fretting, he was
contented with his lot.)
She was in another world where hopes which flew high as
aeroplanes were not supposed to crash –
though she knew better, Mimijune, Julieblossom, with
brothers to protect her, and a green skirt trailing
like a target.
On the island he stopped and started disciplines,
families, shopped around like a spendthrift seeking
value.
And she was giddy in the air, on the ground, trailing her
green skirt like a banner.

He was the old house, the island, hanging learning up to
dry like Nellie's sheets free of salt;
hanging facts and logic on any old dog or cat, draping
philosophies on the passing stranger
(rewriting the history of the world, renaming the children,
the presidents & the gods).
She was separated from partners, each fighting his
battle: the tripping up in London, the slight in
Rome, stale bagels in New York.
She was there, where a telephone to report the crash
didn't work: it was here.
And she is found staggering from a National Park in the
cause of elephant and rhino.

There were those who saw her, green skirt above her head
like the heroine of an Australian film stopping
the traffic;
the same skirt trapped in the door of the car, cruising
(and her brothers, the Generals and Marshals
reverting to type).
Then she was a silver train serving passengers as they
wished; some who saw the mistake

and were patient, read by her light as they entered
    the tunnel which echoed:
Why are the faces of animals expressionless as riddles?
    Where is there *fresh government of bagels*?
And back on the island she would confront an inmate who
    still refused to be bought off with god knows what
    degrees and victories.

4 *(Counting the Letters of)* Love

Haiku

On the verandah
the wet nurse thinks of her own
pomegranate tree

– MIMI KHALVATI

Love Song

And they promised her fire instead of ice
And now last of the brothers comes
For her to melt him

Stone
Wall
Brick

Against her song
This man
Last of the twins

His stone
His wall
His brick

Surviving the body-language of a Sister
Will melt
Under her song

Song about the bell
The fire-
Engine

She is fire-engine
She is bell
From her mouth new sounds

Of metal, furnace, engine
(Not her sounds)
Of boardroom, office, platform

And her face
Is bruised
From the argument

Refusing to change shape
Temperature
The lover

Intact
Traps her metaphors
Into a grammar of ice

And it is so foolish
To train bells and fire-engines
On her own fire

Letter to a Lover, To Be Treated with Suspicion

i

In this rehearsal of complaints,
when there is nothing left to say
and you turn back spurned
by the god of understanding, the god of listening
who this time neglects the quick-change
and inhabits battle-dress
a perfect fit, creased in the right places
in spite of hint of blood and mud,
well then: who could settle for that?
Slow-writing this letter is punishment easier to indulge,
like guilt at the private party
while some outside press and curse,
or are indifferent – we plead time
to get things right. Beyond earshot
wars are lost, and familiar children
seek to bury illusions in their beards.
I have used good years revising
this text, hinting of home, rearranging
furniture, seeing you return from an errand
to space other than this, alien.
Our little drama is too stale for others
pricked by their own needs. Let me not yet
make you visible, let me fail again
to trap features on a sheet cold
as paper. Let me half-answer to four-letter FOOL.

ii

The cudgel coming down misses you,
even now it reeks concern. The cudgel
knarled with logic will make you see mistakes;
self-loading it splays with *logic*
trapped passengers on a train: are they dead?
(Inside he wears the military coat,
fights her in the bush, in the ditch:
how she has changed what he would be?)
I am here with pen, paper and stunned *human*
underground. Do I write this down?
I am a hoarder of experience, I can't
share this. Too late to transfer assets to someone
gone on the early train. Tight-lipped,
I deny this spill of contact.
Here, once again, not knowing, pleased
that it is hard, in motion, with the dead
Bakerloo Line going bluish, greyish, brownish,
hard to think what went before
and us, having no destination in mind, the letter
gets written, gets written. Who is to say
it has travelled in better company?

Blood has been spilt. How to say this *only*
without the quotes of history? That the vein opened to
    accident
makes it no less real, gave it in the high season
the sanctity of marriage earlier than ours,
was a fancy necessary to abandon.
Now blood on earth, on tiles, spasms the night
like the tread (here we go) of an army unaccustomed to
    boots,
like living through the plague of war, Civil
only in name. Though scars heal like new flesh
and disappear on the next generation
these wounds must, we fear, we hope, lurk somewhere.
Sometimes, you do talk nonsense, she says.

iii

You liked it then.
Then I was the athlete giving youth;
surging through long arms
like winning tape, like ribbons in a dream.
Now, fragile, muscly, near-comic
like the man reading a newspaper
in restricted, public space;
like a man with one arm at the urinals
having difficulty . . . need I go on?

Things happened. You hung back and now
eschew words that mean too little, that mean too much:
Germany was devastating, London desolate
was no more than a private headline.
That so much will always live with us
is footnote, no longer text.
Now – we have lost our zest for zest –
you eschew words difficult to say
with honesty, with ease. You eschew eschew.
The jokes are old and deliberate as breaking *eschew*
silence in a sneeze of life.
Time to change the vocabulary.

iv

So you riddle and drown in words, piddle till the sea
is one buoyant wave refusing to break, a cliff of ice
and no one is present to witness this clasp
of man and nature, which won't melt
to flow in the deserts of friendly country;
and here you are, coming from the bathroom, too old to
    be clean,
relieved there is no one to sniff the truth.
Pretend, then, to have a limb in plaster;
a manageable sin, a curable disaster.

I'm the one with the glasses, I say, burdening her
with three decades' absence, turning wife into grandmother
linking not-seeing with the wrong glasses
and other betrayals of flesh growing delicate as yeast.
And I look again at our own dark age, seeking
renaissance, something Carolingian, less brazen
than Florence, survivals a world away of African, Indian
indentured clay shaping foreign interests, nurturing
its own crop: time to reveal our craft. This secret,
logged as bridge across flat country, or a raft
in calm water, in dead sea, a private path
laid down, long abandoned by the enemy,
dishonours your struggle for territory, denies
one other country independence.

In this old rehearsal of complaints
where lines grow long and lose their threat
and we view the world with detachment of reader, of
    viewer – the actor
with a lisp planning to bomb the perfect word,
man who walks in shit on the pavement and doesn't know
    it –
things put on for our entertainment, our diversion
remind us of other selves, here, towards the end of a
    century.

Leaf

and suddenly it was there
a leaf
as in the dream
and those who were surprised
wore smocks smeared with the seasons:
a matching tree would diminish
its moment.
And those in white coats
with bad eyesight
who fought the desert,
brought beauty to fruit and vegetable,
tried to eek mileage
out of the heart,
looked surprised
for the leaf was not intended
(for the rains would bring sadness)
and the tree
the tree
was nowhere.

Rewrite

Beauty screws her new
leg into place and gains
advantage. Blame the limp,
she says, on Progress: who's
for a game then?

                    I'll play,
let me play, says the Beast
sick of being upstaged again.

The hoof in the chest –
a new experience to Beast –
puzzles him: for so long
it had been *his* rôle to give
those beauties pleasure.

Nibble, Nibble

All these yuppie orphans, eager
to be fed – damn,

d'you mind? She removes
the blouse stained

with drink or food
from an OK country:

no guilt there, you see?
As I always say,

can't be too careful
about things these days ...

as competing mouths nibble
nibble at the tips of

there there ... strawbooby
nutsy-wutsy whatsits

from a new garden.

Beast on Holiday

i

After chopping the log
for effect and for firewood,
disturbing white ants, killing
holiday time between breakfast and lunch,
evicting a nation from its olive;
after splintering – damn – old
certainties on a stranger's lawn
he turns to see her (Convent-educated
but no novice) offering pear juice
in a new language, offering
the note of sadness all demand when life
has been sacrificed
to make us comfortable: but there is time
at this retreat to repair damage.

Stray paths weave round the village
where herbs known from shops play
hide-and-seek; talk of nature-nurture
seems in order, and recognition that others –
buongiorno – foreign to the region
have squatters' rights on this favoured hillside.
And then the sound of fire, something red
like wine, like passion of exploding logs
transforms Beast into *il cicisbeo* teasing
from his guitar, song
about her bare feet on the pedals of the car.
And tonight the trip is earned.

ii

Whatever hand I deal
he wins. Other games show him
rising above mere talent,
so we like it here. He has mastered
this scene. From olive grove
to the distant sea, I am climate,
I am Peace in the world.
Like stones here rearranged
into villa, I won't give way (like others?)
to ruin, or slide into the next terrace
and be tragic. I will retain within me hint
of local wines, olive oil, whiff
of the wood-oven – the perfect
second home. I am what keeps him on top,
on top of a pile he thinks stable.
He interprets my smile: 'Your turn:
your turn, my love.'

The Father's Story

HER RED RIB ELK AND EEL HER WET DIP
THE NEW BIB DAZ AND VIM SHE LET RIP
Like a dog smoking a cigarette in his own place
smelling of roses, he needs a new SHE RIB.
Like a god with a clear view of the future
no different from the past, family full of RUT RIB,
slopping yapocking
he will prescribe the ancient JAG RIB:
HER RED RIB ELK AND EEL HER WET DIP
THE NEW BIB DAZ AND VIM SHE LET RIP LET RIP . . .
Wife has not learnt to play the piano: get her a HOE TAG
(now the CAP TAP against her the BOW JAG against her
Sweet Caesar! And there she is on the evening news,
    authentic).
Children TWO SIX TEN up the Everest of Babel they resent
slide into BIG JIG, no CAT FAT sofa table
to land on. And the DAD GOD RAM RIB RAT of all
him say: BIG BAD JET SET AND WAR
him say: SEA SKY MUD MAN AND WAR
and have a nice day, him say

till they come to the scene of my ego-fatigue
stray wife and offspring refusing to grieve
a name now sensuous with mud:
fooey gooey googleey godman: cavalry charge from the old
    stud.
Begetting bastards was long part of the masterplan
to spur this wimp family into a fighting Clan:
    BIG BAD JET SET AND WAR
    SEA SKY MUD MAN AND WAR, Mr President.
And have a nice day.

Love in the Hospital

She slaps him; feels a twinge:
and now he won't hit back. Too weak
to stamp hot anger on her face
he heaves, heaves. She slaps him
perhaps to hurt
more than pride: through blood
and memory he sees her peeling
cardigans, wife-flesh collapsing
heaps in front of strangers.
The shame of it. Nurse. Nurse!
She struggles to remove shirt and trousers
skinning him naked in reproach.
There is no blood. Nurse holds the eye
of an ancient ally, draws back, colludes.
In seconds she has banished
old age, marriage, from her plans.
The other has not lived for this:
this is no payment for life's
submission – though she must return
compliments she was never meant to have.
She slaps him not for the ward's
benefit; and there, damp soft
clay she can't quite mould
through years of fingers going stiff;
and it hurts, the pressure hurts.

The Mother's Tale

So many terrible people are people still
  – GAVIN EWART

Goodness, she said:
Unless you eat this,
Unless you get to bed

The black man
Will get you
And that's worse than

Being dead.
You're all at sea now
In above your head:

The grasping hand
Reaching out to you
From land

Is folly. Just realize
I didn't make you try that one
For size.

He's everything
I promised
Though he won't sing

And dance.
And if he doesn't beat you, well
That's by chance.

I'm truly sorry for being right
Though we must take
Delight

In the buff-
Coloured darlings. Yes,
It's been rough

For all of us,
Determined to meet this setback
Without fuss.

We've been here before
With the Wars and bullies:
It's just a bore

In a home like this
To have brought on
With the bedtime kiss

When this game began
Something rather worse
Than the stock policeman.

Looking Back, Ah, Looking Back

He liked me then
cleaning the window
that gesture

arm
body
me looking up

wiping specks off the glass
like that
– like that?

Ripe tips of me
going their own way, yes
colliding

behind the glass
though I was different then
when I did it

like this
like this
like this

'Little Fellow'

For who's 'tiny' who 'curly'
among those who know them this well?
And a fellow so little inside his pants
astonishes with raw courage
given the chance, as I give it from time to time
to time. For it's a battle to win again
as I wrestle to ground, to sky –
two strong hands and a mouth leading
the attack; though the fellow well-honed
will counter thrusting forward
like sword, like club, blind in attack,
in fury; so I trap and wedge
into any opening near to me, dear to me
lost in me . . . and then to work
drawing the pride, the arrogance
that inflates these little fellows stripped
of cover *brute beast pig* in contest;
till vanquished, he admits, submits . . .
and is once more the household pet,
tail between its legs.

Covering Up

i

For being so broad, this back
Of yours, a target of friendly knives
That do not kill, that carve
Proud stripes on the skin
Like a successful soldier in the wars
We march in support of, and retire wounded;
So, at bedtime the friendly nurse
Can retrace victories, with a mocking finger
As you retell the story of this *Marathon*,
That *Dien Bien Phu* – the *Harrogate* yet to come.
So . . .

This sentence runs longer than your life.
After turning round to face the knives,
To find promise on a face like a new culture
Hard to resist – like the mate you have missed
These lost decades – you stand
Side by side immune
And watch the missiles go past
As no one shoots straight
And wounds of the flesh are curable.

ii

Eyes meet like lovers', the finger
In the mouth trails wisdom like a science, promises
A hand, reprieve, fun.
She is in uniform, wears a mask
And adds a flourish retooling him for love.
And now the mouth is rinsed
And masked and unmasked eyes meet
And the uniform melts
And teeth to last you till the end of life
Bite from the prone position, from the padded chair.

And her name is other than it was.

iii

She will kiss and tell of Eastphalian altarpieces,
With bounty like a new-world language
Part the bush where friends
But no conqueror trod, to rescue you
From your own complacent hand.
And now her children – not your children – born of
    famine
Come up for voyeurs on a screen
While you bluster. And she asks:
Why won't you claim your own?
Why can't you fill our needs?

iv

The pause hints that it is late to call.
Like two nations separated by the same language, these
    jokes
Grow stale late in the century.
The call confirms that lives condemned
To thrive outside books sieve a narrative
Of memory, a husk of dialogue
Beyond last pages.

                    In the Indian restaurant late at night a man
Scans tables till he finds
His double. Hello, and what can we talk about?
Now what has placed us outside human company,
Not the government, woman, war, the threat of Aids:
Let's talk cricket. And what's the latest score?

v

And were you right, my love?
The back is narrower than it was
And yet they find it,
The knives find it. He pretends surprise
That with the smaller target they learn again
To shoot straight.

A Poem of Experience

Happiness, as long as it lasts, is forgetting oneself.
   – FRANÇOIS MITTERRAND

Again I feel that hunger for innocence
No longer raw, quelled now by the memory of feast
And sensation of nights talked away by others.
Here, after the whiff of domestic privilege surrounding
Mixed spice, bay leaf, cinnamon and coriander
I am spun round, as by the call of a vendor in the street
To find myself mistaken: I am facing the other way
Self-conscious and awkward before one, before many
Who have lived lives behind me
And have no need for recruits to their ranks.
So I juggle the option to turn round again, eyes darting
From the wreck of self-image to the threatened blankets
     of Aid.
And I shift expectation till space contracts to fit me
Like these others, living lives behind others.

Far away, smarting from the fist of a malady which loosens
     teeth
And drowns the head in a furnace of screams,
Something crawls from the wreck of the story, uncomforted
By a lover's touch not yet faded, by knowing that broken
     things
Remain fragile. A phantom protects her from the roof of
     the house.
It has travelled so far that countries become its metaphor.
Early camouflage, like a choir in youth which sheltered
     the voice,
Ended like leaves on a desert tree.
It talked of *Guernicas* after Franco, after Picasso;
And was its own government growing into the people; was
     the alchemist
Turning gold into shit: it was a man.
She says this with some rancour, trying to stir taste
Into mixed spice, bay leaf, cinnamon and coriander,
For she too must survive this poem of experience.

The Thing Not Said

We need life-jackets now to float
On words which leave so much unsaid.

How can this not sound like sophistry
To justify absence from your thoughts, your bed?

But this haemorrhaging of language
Still keeps the best phrase locked in my head.

Easy to talk of loneliness, of ageing, damning
Those who would be Presidents and Generals of the dead;

Forgetting the detail, the particular hunger
Of someone you know waiting to be fed.

And now I'm doing it again, drifting on words,
More lines for the simple thing not said.

NOTES

Towards the End of a Century   *pages 16–17*

BRADMAN was never out in the nineties in a Test Match. His Test batting average was 99.94; of major batsmen, Sid Barnes came next with 63.05.

THE THREE W'S: Weekes, Worrell, Walcott – three of the greatest and most devastating stroke-makers ever to appear in the same team. They played for West Indies from 1947 for over a decade.

KANHAI was famous for ending up on his seat after he had swept a four to leg.

'CLIFTON' is Roy Fredericks' middle name. He was a fine, aggressive opening batsman.

LE CORBUSIER and FRANK LLOYD WRIGHT: contrasting architects; the Swiss aggressive, explosive and arrogant in concrete, while Wright's mainly wooden buildings were seen as an unobtrusive extension of the American domestic landscape.

'CHINAMAN': a disguised off-break with leg-break action bowled by a left-handed bowler to a right-handed batsman. This, to a left-hander, is the 'googly'.

A Family Gift   *page 47*

REVERENDS WESLEY AND DE LAWRENCE: John Wesley (1703–1791), one of the founders (with his brother Charles and George Whitefield) of Methodism.

DE LAWRENCE PUBLISHING CO.: purveyor, from America, of mail-order esoteric knowledge, often practised as a supplement to 'church' religion. Influenced some of the founders of Rastafarianism.

WALTER: Walter Rodney (1942–1980), Guyanese historian and political activist; assassinated in Guyana.

MICHAEL: Michael Smith (1954–1983), Jamaican dub poet, murdered in Kingston.

LEGBA: Papa Legba, 'crippled Haitian/Dahomean god of the threshold, of openings', said to guard the gates to the spiritual world.

DRAGON'S TEETH: the name of the house. The 'Dragon's Mouth' is the 20 km channel between Venezuela and Trinidad – so named because of the many teeth-like rocky islets along it, and the strong currents which are a danger to navigation. A London magazine which draws attention to and campaigns against racist/sexist material in children's books is called 'Dragon's Teeth'. Both these geographical and political currents flow into this – perhaps Mediterranean – outpost.

The Grieving   *pages 50–51*

YARD PEOPLE: Often in the Caribbean people congregate in the yard around something communally useful, like a stand-pipe, and gossip. The resulting 'social theatre' has been captured by calypsonians and novelists (C. L. R. James in *Minty Alley*, V. S. Naipaul in *Miguel Street*, Roger Mais in *Brother Man*, Orlando Patterson in *Children of Sisyphus*, etc.).

'Yard Theatre' was also a genre term for early West Indian theatre. A recent anthology of post-independent Jamaican poetry is called *From Our Yard*. In this poem, the sense of 'yard' is somewhat looser. The yard people are those who have made use of the services of the big house – to bake, to wash clothes, to draw water, to borrow utensils of one kind or another, and now lay claim to the abandoned house, in a somewhat disturbing way.

OBEAH (pronounced as two syllables, stressed on the first): magical power.

Olympic Winner, 1988   *page 56*

In 1875, the Englishman Capt. Matthew Webb became the first person to swim the English Channel. He said 'None of the black people that I have ever known approach a first-class English swimmer.' In 1988, B. Nielsen, black, from Surinam, won the Gold Medal in the Men's 200 Metres Butterfly.

Land Behind the Mountains   *page 62*

Looking down on Tirana's Skandebeg Square in the evening reminds one of a Lowry painting. The fact that there are no private cars in Albania helps.

From the Building Site with Love   *page 64*

HOUSE-SLAVE: a rather gross, slow-moving lizard found inside tropical houses, often sheltering in cool spots, bathrooms etc.

Another Footnote, The Same Text   *page 67*

WANTOK: member of the clan (Pidgin).

Beast on Holiday   *page 90*

CICISBEO: married Italian woman's male companion or lover.

By E. A. Markham from Anvil

HUMAN RITES

All aspects of E. A. Markham's range are represented in this selection of his poetry from 1970–82: explorations of his West Indian background, love poems, poems on historical, social and political themes, and the special brand of ironic humour in his 'Lambchops' poems, as effective on the page as they are in his own performance.

LIVING IN DISGUISE

In the first part of this collection in three voices, Markham is unmasked as Sally Goodman, feminist poet of the 1970s. His previously known alias, Paul St Vincent – social satirist, performance poet and creator of 'Lambchops' – is also featured. Many of the poems as E. A. Markham draw on his experience in Papua New Guinea during 1983–85.

'All three of these creators are on good form.'

– PETER PORTER in *The Observer*

Some comments on E. A. Markham's poetry

'Markham's writing is witty, varied, imaginative and sometimes provocative ... one of the most entertaining poets around these days.'

– JIM BURNS in *Ambit*

'Markham is indeed a bold writer.... A thinker rather than a describer, who credits the reader with an intelligence equal to his own, he has developed into a political writer in the best (not necessarily widest) sense.'

– CAROL RUMENS in *TLS*

'An able and indeed fascinating poet. His longer poems, under his own name, are full of wonderful material.'

– GEORGE SZIRTES in *The Poetry Review*